WAY

I0643942

JUN 06

THE CHICAGO WHITE SOX

BY

MARK STEWART

Content Consultant
James L. Gates, Jr.
Library Director
National Baseball Hall of Fame and Museum

NORWOOD HOUSE PRESS

CHICAGO, ILLINOIS

Norwood House Press
P.O. Box 316598
Chicago, Illinois 60631

For information regarding Norwood House Press, please visit our website at:
www.norwoodhousepress.com or call 866-565-2900.

All photos courtesy of AP/Wide World Photos, Inc. except the following:
F.W. Rueckheim & Brother (6 & 34 top right), Exhibit Supply Co. (7 & 39), Gum Inc. (14),
Author's Collection (16, 17 bottom, 34 top left and bottom right & 41),
Sweet Caporal (17 top & 20), Topps, Inc. (29, 40 & 41), The Sporting News (34 bottom left),
Bowman Gum Co. (35 left), Red Heart Dog Food (43).
Special thanks to Topps, Inc.

Editor: Mike Kennedy
Designer: Ron Jaffe
Project Management: Black Book Partners, LLC.

Special thanks to Bobby Hall, and Pam and Richard Donath.

Library of Congress Cataloging-in-Publication Data

Stewart, Mark, 1960-
  The Chicago White Sox / Mark Stewart ; content consultant, James L.
Gates, Jr.
      p. cm. -- (Team spirit)
    Summary: "Presents the history, accomplishments and key personalities of
the Chicago White Sox baseball team. Includes timelines, quotes, maps,
glossary and websites"--Provided by publisher.
    Includes bibliographical references and index.
    ISBN-13: 978-1-59953-060-4 (library edition : alk. paper)
    ISBN-10: 1-59953-060-0 (library edition : alk. paper) 1. Chicago White
Sox (Baseball team)--History--Juvenile literature. I. Gates, Jr., James L. II.
Title. III. Series.
  GV875.C58S83 2006
  796.357'640977311--dc22
                                                    2005035878

Manufactured in the United States of America.

COVER PHOTO: The White Sox celebrate after winning
the 2005 American League pennant.

Table of Contents

SPORTS WORDS & VOCABULARY WORDS: In this book, you will find many words that are new to you. You may also see familiar words used in new ways. The glossary on page 46 gives the meanings of baseball words, as well as "everyday" words that have special baseball meanings. These words appear in **bold type** throughout the book. The glossary on page 47 gives the meanings of vocabulary words that are not related to baseball. They appear in ***bold italic type*** throughout the book.

Meet the White Sox

Have you ever watched baseball players come to work at the stadium before a game? In most cities, they act like **glamorous** celebrities. They walk and talk like movie stars. The Chicago White Sox are different. They are not so easy to pick out of a crowd. In fact, they look a lot like the fans who come to watch them play.

Those fans mean a lot to the White Sox. The team has been competing for Chicago's baseball heart for more than 100 years. They play the game hard, and they enjoy their victories as much as the people in the stands do. If you play for the White Sox, this is one of the first things you learn—the fans are a huge part of the team.

This book tells the story of the White Sox. They have had many ups and downs in their history, but their **formula** for winning has never changed. When they hit, throw, and catch the baseball—and hold nothing back—good things usually happen. It may not be the glamorous way to play. But it is definitely the White Sox way.

Jermaine Dye and Paul Konerko get high fives as they enter the Chicago dugout. Both runners scored after Konerko hit a home run against the Boston Red Sox in a 2005 playoff game.

Way Back When

The 1901 season was an exciting one for Chicago baseball fans. A new league—the **American League (A.L.)**—was born, and its best team played in the city. They were named the White Stockings, but soon everyone was calling them the White Sox. They were owned by a man named Charles Comiskey. He had been a star first baseman in the 1880s.

Chicago's **National League (N.L.)** team was not happy to have a rival. They made the White Sox agree to play their games far away, on Chicago's South Side. The White Sox still call this part of the city "home."

The White Sox played exciting baseball. They stole a lot of bases, and used the **hit-and-run** play whenever they could. Their pitching was good and their fielding was even better. At the end of the A.L.'s first season, they were league champions. Over the years,

COMISKEY, OWNER OF WHITE SOX

Charles Comiskey,
the first owner of the White Sox.

the White Sox were usually at their best
when they played the game this way.

The White Sox had some of baseball's
greatest players in the early years of the
20th century. Their stars included Ed
Walsh, Eddie Cicotte, Ray Schalk, Eddie
Collins, George Davis, Fielder Jones,
Oscar "Happy" Felsch, and Joe Jackson.
The White Sox won the **World Series** in
1906 and 1917, but their best team was
the one that captured the **pennant** in 1919. No one could believe it
when the White Sox lost the World Series that fall. Later, it was
discovered that several members of the team had made bad plays on
purpose. These players were thrown out of baseball forever, and the
1919 team is still called the "Black Sox" by the fans.

During the 1920s, 1930s, and 1940s, a handful of stars wore the
Chicago uniform, including pitchers Red Faber and Ted Lyons, and
hitters Bibb Falk and Luke Appling. But it was not until the 1950s that
the White Sox had a team good enough to challenge for the A.L.

pennant again. Led by infielders Nellie Fox and Luis Aparicio, and pitchers Early Wynn and Billy Pierce, the White Sox finally made it back to the World Series in 1959, but they lost to the Los Angeles Dodgers.

Amazingly, it would take more than 40 years before the White Sox were good enough to play in the World Series again. Even so, they had some of baseball's most *remarkable* players during that time, including Wilbur Wood, Dick Allen, Harold Baines, Carlton Fisk, Ozzie Guillen, and Frank Thomas. Yet the White Sox always seemed to be missing something. In the end, it would take a lesson from the past to show the team the way to its future.

TOP: Harold Baines, the leader of the White Sox during the 1980s.
LEFT: Luis Aparicio, the shortstop on Chicago's 1959 pennant-winning team.

The Team Today

During the 1990s, the White Sox tried to find powerful hitters who could win games with home runs. This made White Sox games fun to watch, but often it was the visiting team's **sluggers** who hit the game-winning home runs. Year after year, Chicago would fall short of its goal of winning the pennant.

Finally, the White Sox decided to go back to a formula that had succeeded in the past. They built a team full of players who worked hard to get hits and walks, and who never missed an opportunity to take an extra base. The White Sox put steady fielders at the different positions, and found good, smart pitchers who learned how to win close games.

In 2005, the White Sox finished the season with the most victories in the A.L. Few people believed that they would continue to win with this new style of play, but they defeated the Red Sox and Angels in the **playoffs** to reach the World Series. After beating the Houston Astros four games to none, the White Sox were world champions for the first time since 1917!

Catcher A.J. Pierzynski leaps into the arms of pitcher Bobby Jenks after the final out of the 2005 World Series. Third baseman Joe Crede is ready to join the fun.

11

Home Turf

The White Sox play their games at U.S. Cellular Field, which many fans call "new Comiskey Park." The stadium opened on April 18, 1991. This is the third home for the team. Their first stadium was called South Side Park. The White Sox played there until 1910, when the team moved to Comiskey Park. It was called the "Baseball Palace of the World," then renamed after the team's owner, Charles Comiskey. They stayed there for 81 years.

The current stadium is located right across the street from the site of "old" Comiskey Park. It has the look and feel of an old-time stadium. The scoreboard *erupts* with fireworks when the White Sox win an important game. All of the seats in the stadium offer a great view of the field. White Sox fans enjoy the stadium, and show it by cheering as loud as any fans in baseball.

U.S. CELLULAR FIELD BY THE NUMBERS

- *The stadium has 39,336 seats.*
- *The distance from home plate to the left field foul pole is 330 feet.*
- *The distance from home plate to the center field wall is 400 feet.*
- *The distance from home plate to the right field foul pole is 335 feet.*
- *The stadium includes one very popular feature from the old Comiskey Park—outside showers for hot days.*

The White Sox practice before Game One of the 2005 World Series.

Dressed for Success

The White Sox have worn many different uniform designs since their first season. Most have included the word "Chicago," the letter C, or the word "Sox." The first time fans saw "Sox" on the team's uniform was in 1910. The team actually wore all-white socks until 1946. In 1960, the White Sox became the first team to put player names on the backs of their uniforms. In 1967, the team's road uniform spelled out "Chicago White Sox." This was one of the few times a baseball team has used its entire name on a uniform.

During the past 40 years, the White Sox have experimented with some fun ideas. In the 1960s, the team started wearing powder-blue uniforms on the road. In the 1970s, the White Sox actually wore red socks for a couple of seasons. In the 1980s, the team tried a

modern look, with "Sox" spelled out in big lettering on their caps and jerseys, and numbers on their pants. In recent years, the White Sox started using black as an important uniform color. The fans like this uniform, because it makes their players look tough.

Taft Wright models the team's uniform from the early 1940s.

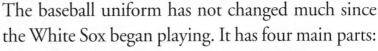

The baseball uniform has not changed much since the White Sox began playing. It has four main parts:

- a cap or batting helmet with a sun visor;
- a top with a player's number on the back;
- pants that reach down between the ankle and the knee;
- stirrup-style socks.

The uniform top sometimes has a player's name on the back. The team's name, city, or *logo* is usually on the front. Baseball teams wear light-colored uniforms when they play at home, and darker styles when they play on the road.

For more than 100 years, baseball uniforms were made of wool *flannel* and were very baggy. This helped the sweat *evaporate* and gave players the freedom to move around. Today's uniforms are made of *synthetic* fabrics that stretch with players and keep them dry and cool.

Jon Garland throws a pitch in Chicago's home uniform.

We Won!

The White Sox won the World Series three times during a 100-year period. They were crowned champions of baseball in 1906, 1917, and 2005. Although the game changed a lot during this time, the Chicago teams that won these three World Series were actually quite similar. Each club had good pitching, fine defense, **aggressive** base-runners, and hitters who were at their best under pressure.

The 1906 World Series was the only one ever played between Chicago's two teams, the White Sox and Cubs. The Cubs had set a record by winning 116 games during the season, and were expected to win easily. The White Sox were managed by Fielder Jones, a man who studied baseball like a science. He knew that he had to do something unusual to beat the Cubs.

WALSH, CHICAGO AMER.

Twice in this series, Jones handed the ball to a young pitcher name Ed Walsh. Walsh threw a **spitball**—a pitch that squirted out of his fingers like a watermelon seed, and then moved suddenly as it neared home plate. The Cubs were helpless against Walsh, who won two games and struck out 17 batters. The White Sox split the other four games with the Cubs, and won the World Series four games to two.

The White Sox played the New York Giants in the 1917 World Series. Both teams had good hitting and pitching, so it was no surprise when fielding turned out to be the big difference in their games. Chicago fans cheered as their stars—including Joe Jackson, Ray Schalk, and Eddie Collins—made one great defensive play after another. Red Faber and Eddie Cicotte gave the White Sox all the pitching they needed to win four games to two.

The White Sox won the A.L. pennant in 1919 and 1959, but lost in the World Series both times.

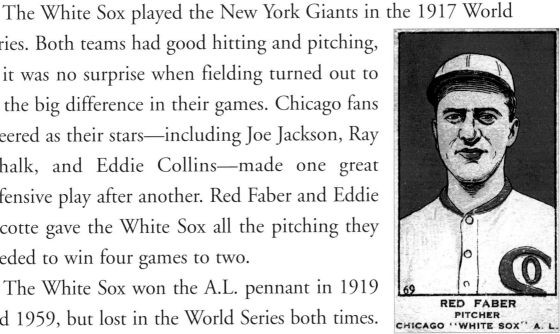

69
RED FABER
PITCHER
CHICAGO "WHITE SOX" A. L.

In 1983, they won the A.L.'s **West Division**, but lost to the Baltimore Orioles in the **American League Championship Series (ALCS)**. The White Sox made it to the playoffs again in 1993 and 2000, but could not win the pennant either time.

The 2005 White Sox finally made it to the World Series. Like the great Chicago teams of the past, they had several talented pitchers, including Mark Buehrle, Jon Garland, Freddy Garcia, Jose Contreras, and Bobby Jenks. They also had very good fielders, including Aaron Rowand, Joe Crede, and Juan Uribe. All year long, the team got important hits from Paul Konerko, Scott Podsednik, and Jermaine Dye.

The White Sox met the Houston Astros in the World Series and played four very close games. Chicago *prevailed* in all of them, including a 14-inning victory in Game Three and a spine-tingling 1–0 win in Game Four. For the third time in a century, the old formula for success worked once again—pitching plus defense plus timely hitting equaled a championship.

ABOVE: The White Sox celebrate after winning the 2005 World Series in Houston.   **RIGHT**: Jose Contreras fires a pitch against the Astros in the 2005 World Series.

Go-To Guys

To be a true star in baseball, you need more than a quick bat and a strong arm. You have to be a "go-to guy"—someone the manager wants on the pitcher's mound or in the batter's box when it matters most. White Sox fans have had a lot to cheer about over the years, including these great stars…

THE PIONEERS

ED WALSH   Pitcher

- BORN: 5/14/1881   • DIED: 5/26/1959
- PLAYED FOR TEAM: 1904 TO 1916

Ed Walsh was the first player who learned how to control the spitball, a pitch that was tricky to throw and almost impossible to hit. He won 40 games for the White Sox in 1908, and led the A.L. in strikeouts twice. The spitball was outlawed in 1920 because it was dangerous to batters.

EDDIE COLLINS   Second Baseman

- BORN: 5/2/1887   • DIED: 3/25/1951   • PLAYED FOR TEAM: 1915 TO 1926

Eddie Collins was known for his **sportsmanship** at a time when baseball was a very rough game. He was also one of the best base-stealers and bunters who ever lived. The more competitive the situation, the better Collins played.

ABOVE: Ed Walsh

TED LYONS   Pitcher

• BORN: 12/28/1900   • DIED: 7/25/1986   • PLAYED FOR TEAM: 1923 TO 1946

Ted Lyons threw a fastball that moved as the batter started his swing. He mixed this pitch with a **knuckleball** to win 260 games.

LUKE APPLING   Shortstop

• BORN: 4/2/1907   • DIED: 1/3/1991   • PLAYED FOR TEAM: 1930 TO 1950

Luke Appling was an expert at hitting foul balls. He would stay at bat until he earned a walk, or until the pitcher gave him a good pitch to hit. Appling was the A.L.'s top hitter twice.

MINNIE MINOSO   Outfielder

• BORN: 11/29/1922

• PLAYED FOR TEAM: 1951 TO 1957, 1960 TO 1961, 1964, 1976 & 1980

Minnie Minoso led the A.L. in stolen bases his first three years with Chicago, and made the **All-Star** team six times as a member of the White Sox.

NELLIE FOX   Second Baseman

• BORN: 12/25/1927   • DIED: 12/1/1975   • PLAYED FOR TEAM: 1950 TO 1963

Nellie Fox was a great fielder and base-runner, and one of the hardest men in history to strike out. He was the A.L.'s **Most Valuable Player (MVP)** in 1959.

LUIS APARICIO   Shortstop

• BORN: 4/29/1934   • PLAYED FOR TEAM: 1956 TO 1962 AND 1968 TO 1970

Luis Aparicio was a *superb* fielder and daring runner. He led the A.L. in stolen bases in his first seven seasons with Chicago.

MODERN STARS

HAROLD BAINES   Outfielder/Designated Hitter

- BORN: 3/15/1959
- PLAYED FOR TEAM: 1980 TO 1989, 1996 TO 1997, AND 2000 TO 2001

Harold Baines was the first player chosen in the 1977 baseball **draft**, and he rewarded the White Sox with many great seasons. He became the first White Sox player to hit 20 home runs six years in a row. Baines was at his best while hitting with runners on base.

CARLTON FISK   Catcher

- BORN: 12/26/1947   • PLAYED FOR TEAM: 1981 TO 1993

When Carlton Fisk joined the White Sox at the age of 33, many fans thought he only had a few good seasons left. He led the team to a division title in 1983, then caught for 10 more seasons. Fisk hit more than 200 home runs during his time in Chicago.

OZZIE GUILLEN   Shortstop

- BORN: 1/20/1964   • PLAYED FOR TEAM: 1985 TO 1997

Ozzie Guillen was one of the team's most popular and exciting players. He found ways to win games that did not always show up in his statistics, but no one ever doubted his value. Guillen later managed Chicago to a championship.

ABOVE: Harold Baines   **TOP RIGHT**: Frank Thomas
BOTTOM RIGHT: Paul Konerko

FRANK THOMAS

First Baseman/ Designated Hitter

- BORN: 5/27/1968   • PLAYED FOR TEAM: 1990 TO 2005

Frank Thomas joined the White Sox in 1990, and it did not take long for him to become the greatest hitter in the team's history. He batted over .300 eight years in a row, and was voted the A.L.'s MVP in 1993 and 1994.

MARK BUEHRLE

Pitcher

- BORN: 3/23/1979   • FIRST YEAR WITH TEAM: 2000

When Mark Buehrle joined Chicago's **starting rotation** in 2001, he gave the White Sox a pitcher they could count on every time he walked to the mound. Buehrle became the first starter ever to earn a win in one World Series game and a **save** in the next.

PAUL KONERKO

First Baseman

- BORN: 3/5/1976   • FIRST YEAR WITH TEAM: 1999

Paul Konerko proved that good guys finish first when he helped the White Sox win the 2005 World Series. He brought a powerful bat and a great sense of humor to the team in 1999, and soon became a leader in the Chicago dugout.

On the Sidelines

The White Sox have had some of the smartest men in baseball guiding their team. Charles Comiskey, the team's first owner, was the most powerful owner in the American League for many years. Bill Veeck was another owner of the White Sox. He knew how to put good players on the field, and how to keep fans entertained in their seats.

The White Sox have had many good managers, including Fielder Jones, Clarence "Pants" Rowland, William "Kid" Gleason, Jimmie Dykes, Paul Richards, Tony LaRussa, Jeff Torborg, and Jerry Manuel. One of the best was Al Lopez, who led the team to the pennant in 1959. Lopez was a former catcher. He was an expert at getting the best performances out of his pitchers.

In 2004, the White Sox hired Ozzie Guillen to manage the team. He was one of the most beloved players in the team's history. When Guillen changed the team's focus from power hitting to pitching and defense, many fans wondered if he knew what he was doing. They had their answer a year later, when the White Sox won the World Series.

Ozzie Guillen brought enthusiasm and a sharp baseball mind to the White Sox.

One Great Day

When the White Sox beat the Houston Astros 5–3 in the opening game of the 2005 World Series, the players were *ecstatic*. Manager Ozzie Guillen did not want his players to get too excited, however. The Astros were a dangerous opponent, so the White Sox needed to stay focused and win Game Two to take control of the series.

The Astros fought hard to tie the series. They were leading 5–2 in the seventh inning of Game Two when the White Sox came to bat. Juan Uribe and Tadahito Iguchi reached base, then Jermaine Dye was hit by a pitch to load the bases. The next batter, Paul Konerko, saw a pitch he liked and ripped it into the seats for a **grand slam**. Chicago now led 6–5, but Houston tied the score in the top of the ninth inning.

In the bottom of the ninth inning, the White Sox sent Scott Podsednik to the plate. He was one of the fastest players on the team, but he was not very powerful. In fact, Podsednik did not hit one home run during the season. Houston's pitcher, Brad Lidge,

Scott Podsednik crushes a Brad Lidge fastball for the winning hit in Game Two.

wanted Podsednik to hit the ball in the air, where his speed would not be an advanta)ge.

Lidge fired a pitch right down the middle. Podsednik took a smooth swing and his bat met the ball just right. It soared toward centerfield, and for a moment Lidge thought he had won the battle. But the ball kept going and going—right over the fence, for a game-winning home run!

Podsednik could not believe it. He grinned like a little boy as he ran around the bases, and jumped into the arms of his teammates, who were waiting for him at home plate. The White Sox were 7–6 winners, and went on to win the World Series.

Legend Has It

Did Martians kidnap the team's two best players in 1959?

LEGEND HAS IT that they did. Fans at Comiskey Park watched in amazement as a helicopter landed on the field and four tiny actors in Martian costumes hopped out. They made their way to the White Sox dugout and took Nellie Fox and Luis Aparicio prisoner, with ray guns disguised as baseball bats. It was all a joke, of course—another *publicity stunt* by the team's owner, Bill Veeck.

Did Jim Rivera refuse a baseball autographed by president John F. Kennedy?

LEGEND HAS IT that he did. On Opening Day in 1961, the White Sox star caught the season's *traditional* "first pitch" by president Kennedy before a game in Washington, D.C. Rivera asked Kennedy for his autograph on the ball, but took one look at it and gave it back to the president. "You'll have to do better than that, John," Rivera said. "This is a scribble—I can hardly read it."

Was White Sox ace Mark Buehrle really cut from his high school baseball team?

LEGEND HAS IT that he was—not once, but twice! Mark Dunahue, the head coach of Francis Howell North in Missouri, liked the young pitcher. But his assistant coaches **cut** him as a freshman and again as a sophomore. Four years later, Buehrle was pitching in the big leagues for the White Sox—and even struck out Alex Rodriguez in the playoffs. Coach Dunahue now makes all of the final cuts himself—he calls it the "Buehrle Rule."

LEFT: A quartet of "Martians" enters the Chicago dugout.
ABOVE: Jim Rivera

It Really Happened

In 1976, the White Sox were bought by baseball's greatest *showman*, Bill Veeck. Veeck had owned the team once before and they had done very well under his leadership. When he returned in 1976, he believed that the White Sox had become boring. Veeck promised fans that he would make Chicago baseball fun again.

One of the first things Veeck did was to order different uniforms. When the players and fans saw the new design, they could not believe their eyes. No baseball team had ever worn anything like them. Nothing seemed to match anything else.

The caps spelled out "Sox" in futuristic lettering. The uniform tops had no buttons—they were pullover jerseys that were meant to be worn outside the pants, like pajamas. They had v-neck collars with flaps, which looked like a mix of 1870s and 1970s styles. The lettering on these tops did not match the caps—it looked like it was from the turn of the century.

No one knew what to make of the team's new uniform. But Veeck was not finished yet. On hot days, he had his players wear shorts! They may have been cooler than traditional baseball pants, but they were no fun to slide in—ouch! Just as painful were the jokes opponents made about the Chicago players' knobby knees.

Bill Veeck and five former White Sox unveil Chicago's 1976 uniforms.
Bill Skowron and Moe Drabowski wear the home whites,
Dave Nicholson and Dan Osinski wear the dark road
styles, and Jim Rivera models the team's famous shorts.

Veeck could see how unhappy his players were, so he told them they did not have to wear the shorts anymore. He was disappointed that his experiment failed, but deep down he still believed that his 1976 uniform was the wave of the future.

Team Spirit

When the White Sox won the 2005 World Series, they were playing in Houston, Texas. That did not keep fans in Chicago from celebrating. Thousands of people—many with tears streaming down their faces—poured into the streets to rejoice in their team's long-awaited victory. When you wait more than 80 years to win a championship, it is okay to cry.

The biggest party in town took place in the United Center, a basketball and hockey arena. Thousands of fans gathered there to watch the game on the large television monitors. When they left the arena, they looked up at the statue of basketball star Michael Jordan and smiled. Someone had put a White Sox jersey on him!

On Chicago's South Side, fans met outside the team's stadium to celebrate. Their sidewalk party went on so late that a night watchman finally had to beg them to go home. And for many hours, the bells of the Nativity of Our Lord church clanged the notes to "Go Go Go White Sox"—the theme of Chicago's 1959 pennant-winning club.

The White Sox are showered with ticker tape during the parade to celebrate their 2005 championship.

Timeline

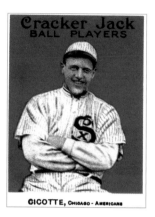

Eddie Cicotte, one of the players who "fixed" the 1919 World Series.

1901
The team wins the first American League pennant.

1919
Eight Chicago players are involved in a plot with gamblers to lose the World Series.

EDDIE COLLINS
2nd B.—Chicago White Sox
33

Eddie Collins

1917
Eddie Collins leads the White Sox over the New York Giants in the World Series.

1925
Ted Lyons leads the A.L. with 21 wins and five **shutouts**.

1959
The White Sox win the pennant but lose to the Los Angeles Dodgers in the World Series.

Ted Lyons

Minnie
Minoso

Frank
Thomas

1980
57-year-old coach Minnie Minoso is
activated by the team and plays two games.

1994
Frank Thomas wins his
second MVP in a row.

1976
The White Sox
wear uniforms that
include shorts.

1983
The White Sox win
their first division title.

2005
The White Sox beat
the Houston Astros to
win the World Series.

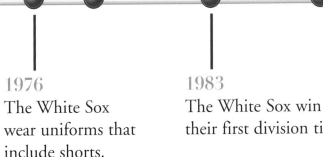

Tadahito Iguchi and Jermaine Dye
celebrate after scoring in Game
Three of the 2005 World Series.

Fun Facts

HITLESS IN CHICAGO

The 1906 White Sox won the world championship despite a team batting average of .230 and just seven home runs. They were nicknamed the "Hitless Wonders."

RECORD BREAKERS

In 1979, the White Sox asked fans to bring their least favorite disco records to the stadium. They planned to blow them up between games of a **doubleheader**. So many fans showed up for "Disco Demolition Night" that the crowd could not be controlled, and the White Sox were forced to **forfeit** the second game.

DUCK AND COVER

When the White Sox won the pennant in 1959, Fire Commissioner Bob Quinn ordered the city's sirens to be sounded to celebrate. Unfortunately, thousands of people thought that the sirens meant a nuclear attack was coming!

PRETTY GOOD

The 1983 White Sox played a lot better than they looked. Several players grew their hair long, went days without shaving, and loved wearing dirty caps and uniforms. The team's battle cry that year was "Winning Ugly!" And they did—the White Sox won 99 times, more than any other team in baseball.

NEW SOX, OLD SOX

In 1956, 16-year-old Jim Derrington pitched a game for the White Sox. He was the youngest pitcher in league history. In 1976 and 1980, the team activated their beloved coach, Minnie Minoso. That made Minoso (who was 57 in 1980) the only man ever to play in five different *decades*—the 1940s, '50s, '60s, '70s, and '80s.

LEFT: Fans run wild on "Disco Demolition Night."
TOP: LaMarr Hoyt, the leading pitcher on the 1983 White Sox.
RIGHT: The White Sox coaches watch young Jim Derrington.

Talking Baseball

Mark Buehrle

"I just go out there, throw strikes, and give my team a chance to win."

—*Mark Buehrle,*
on the secret to
being a successful
pitcher

"I don't think anyone ever liked to play more than I did."

—*Nellie Fox, on*
why he played
hard every inning
of every game

"Being **patient** is something that's easy to say and hard to do. But if you can do it, the pitcher eventually has to come to you."

—Frank Thomas, on waiting for a good pitch to hit

"You can't let any team awe you. If you do, you'll wind up a lousy player."

—Luke Appling, on standing up to a talented opponent

Luke Appling

"Do what you love to do and give it your very best. Whether it's business or baseball, or the theater, or any field. If you don't love what you're doing and you can't give it your best, get out of it."

—Al Lopez, on choosing a career

For the Record

The great White Sox teams and players have left their marks on the record books. These are the "best of the best"…

Nellie Fox

DICK
ALLEN
CHICAGO WHITE SOX   1st BASE

Dick Allen

WHITE SOX AWARD WINNERS

WINNER	AWARD	YEAR
Luis Aparicio	Rookie of the Year*	1956
Nellie Fox	Most Valuable Player	1959
Early Wynn	Cy Young Award**	1959
Gary Peters	Rookie of the Year	1963
Tommie Agee	Rookie of the Year	1966
Dick Allen	Most Valuable Player	1972
LaMarr Hoyt	Cy Young Award	1983
Ron Kittle	Rookie of the Year	1983
Tony LaRussa	Manager of the Year	1983
Ozzie Guillen	Rookie of the Year	1985
Jeff Torborg	Manager of the Year	1990
Jack McDowell	Cy Young Award	1993
Frank Thomas	Most Valuable Player	1993
Frank Thomas	Most Valuable Player	1994
Jerry Manuel	Manager of the Year	2000
Ozzie Guillen	Manager of the Year	2005
Jermaine Dye	World Series MVP	2005

* The Rookie of the Year award award is given to the league's best first-year player.
** The Cy Young award is given to the league's best pitcher each year.

WHITE SOX ACHIEVEMENTS

ACHIEVEMENT	YEAR
A.L. Pennant Winner	1901
A.L. Pennant Winner	1906
World Series Champions	1906
A.L. Pennant Winner	1917
World Series Champions	1917
A.L. Pennant Winner	1919
A.L. Pennant Winner	1959
A.L. Pennant Winner	2005
World Series Champions	2005

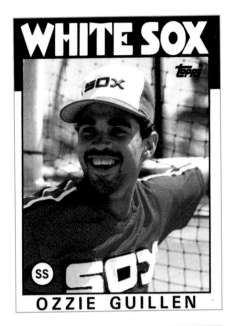

WHITE SOX

OZZIE GUILLEN

TOP: Ozzie Guillen is pictured in his rookie season with the White Sox.

RIGHT: Fielder Jones, wearing the team's famous white socks, meets with Cubs' manager Frank Chance and umpires before a 1906 World Series game.

Pinpoints

The history of a baseball team is made up of many smaller stories. These stories take place all over the map—not just in the city a team calls "home." Match the push-pins on these maps to the Team Facts and you will begin to see the story of the White Sox unfold!

TEAM FACTS

1 Chicago, Illinois—*The White Sox have played here since 1901.*

2 Detroit, Michigan—*Billy Pierce was born here.*

3 St. Thomas, Pennsylvania—*Nellie Fox was born here.*

4 New York, New York—*The White Sox won the 1917 World Series here.*

5 Easton, Maryland—*Harold Baines was born here.*

6 Columbus, Georgia—*Frank Thomas was born here.*

7 Tampa, Florida—*Al Lopez was born here.*

8 Houston, Texas—*The White Sox won the 2005 World Series here.*

9 Valencia, California—*Jon Garland was born here.*

10 Tokyo, Japan—*Tadahido Iguchi was born here.*

11 Ocumare del Tuy, Venezuela—*Ozzie Guillen was born here.*

12 Las Martinas, Cuba—*Jose Contreras was born here.*

Billy Pierce

43

Play Ball

Baseball is a game played between two teams over nine innings. Teams take one turn at bat and one turn in the field during each inning. A turn at bat ends when three outs are made. The batters on the hitting team try to reach base safely. The players on the fielding team try to prevent this from happening.

In baseball, the ball is controlled by the pitcher. The pitcher must throw the ball to the batter, who decides whether or not to swing at each pitch. If a batter swings and misses, it is a strike. If the batter lets a good pitch go by, it is also a strike. If the batter swings and the ball does not stay in fair territory (between the v-shaped lines that begin at home plate) it is called "foul," and is counted as a strike. If the pitcher throws three strikes, the batter is out. If the pitcher throws four bad pitches before that, the batter is awarded first base. This is called a base-on-balls, or "walk."

When the batter swings the bat and hits the ball, everyone springs into action. If a fielder catches a batted ball before it hits the ground, the batter is out. If a fielder scoops the ball off the ground and throws it to first base before the batter arrives, the batter is out. If the batter reaches first base safely, he is credited with a hit. A one-base hit is called a single, a two-base hit is called a double, a three-base hit is called a triple, and a four-base hit is called a home run.

Runners who reach base are only safe when they are touching one of the bases. If they are caught between the bases, the fielders can tag them with the ball and record an out.

A batter who is able to circle the bases and make it back to home plate before three outs are made is credited with a run scored. The team with the most runs after nine innings is the winner.

Anyone who has played baseball (or softball) knows that it can be a complicated game. Every player on the field has a job to do. Different players have different strengths and weaknesses. The pitchers, batters, and managers make hundreds of decisions every game. The more you play and watch baseball, the more "little things" you are likely to notice. The next time you are at a game, look for these plays:

PLAY LIST

DOUBLE PLAY—A play where the fielding team is able to make two outs on one batted ball. This usually happens when a runner is on first base, and the batter hits a ground ball to one of the infielders. The base runner is forced out at second base and the ball is then thrown to first base before the batter arrives.

HIT AND RUN—A play where the runner on first base sprints to second base while the pitcher is throwing the ball to the batter. When the second baseman or shortstop moves toward the base to wait for the catcher's throw, the batter tries to hit the ball to the place that the fielder has just left. If the batter swings and misses, the fielding team can tag the runner out.

INTENTIONAL WALK—A play when the pitcher throws four bad pitches on purpose, allowing the batter to walk to first base. This happens when the pitcher would much rather face the next batter—and is willing to risk putting a runner on base.

SACRIFICE BUNT—A play where the batter makes an out on purpose so that a teammate can move to the next base. On a bunt, the batter tries to "deaden" the pitch with the bat instead of swinging at it.

SHOESTRING CATCH—A play where an outfielder catches a short hit an inch or two above the ground, near the tops of his shoes. It is not easy to run as fast as you can and lower your glove without slowing down. It can be risky, too. If a fielder misses a shoestring catch, the ball might roll all the way to the fence.

Glossary

BASEBALL WORDS TO KNOW

ACTIVATED—Made an official player.

ALL-STAR— A player who is selected to play in baseball's annual All-Star Game.

AMERICAN LEAGUE (A.L.)—One of the two major leagues. The A.L. began play in 1901.

AMERICAN LEAGUE CHAMPIONSHIP SERIES (ALCS)—The series that determines which A.L. team will advance to the World Series.

CUT—Taken off a team.

DOUBLEHEADER—Two games in one day, played with a short break in between. In the early days of baseball, most teams played doubleheaders on Sundays.

DRAFT—The annual meeting at which baseball teams take turns choosing the best high-school and college players.

FORFEIT—Lose by breaking the rules.

GRAND SLAM—A home run with the bases loaded.

HIT-AND-RUN—A play executed by the team at bat (see page 45).

KNUCKLEBALL—A pitch thrown with no spin, which "wobbles" as it nears home plate. A knuckleball is held with the tips of the fingers, so the batter sees a pitcher's knuckles.

MOST VALUABLE PLAYER (MVP)—An award given each year to the league's top player; an MVP is also selected for the World Series and All-Star Game.

NATIONAL LEAGUE (N.L.)—The older of the two major leagues; the N.L. began play in 1876.

PENNANT—A league championship. The term comes from the triangular flag awarded to each season's champion, beginning in the 1870s.

PLAYOFFS—The games played after the regular season to determine which teams will advance to the World Series.

SAVE —A statistic relief pitchers earn when they get the final out of a close game.

SHUTOUTS —Games in which one team does not allow its opponent to score a run.

SLUGGERS—Powerful hitters.

SPITBALL—A pitch thrown with slippery fingers, which swerves suddenly as it nears home plate. The spitball was outlawed in 1920.

SPORTSMANSHIP— The good behavior someone should show when playing a sport or game.

STARTING ROTATION—The group of pitchers who take turns beginning games for their team.

WEST DIVISION—A group of teams (within a league) that play in the western part of the country; the White Sox were in the A.L. West from 1969 to 1992, and have been in the A.L. Central since 1993.

WORLD SERIES—The world championship series played between the winners of the National League and American League.

OTHER WORDS TO KNOW

AGGRESSIVE—Acting boldly or powerfully.

DECADES—Ten-year periods.

ECSTATIC—Feeling great joy.

ERUPTS—Bursts suddenly.

EVAPORATE—Disappear, or turn into vapor.

FLANNEL—A soft wool or cotton material.

FORMULA—A set way of doing something.

GLAMOROUS—Exciting and charming.

LOGO—A symbol or design that represents a company or team.

PATIENT—Able to wait calmly.

PREVAILED—Won.

PUBLICITY STUNT—An unusual act or event done to draw the attention of the public.

REMARKABLE—Unusual or exceptional.

SHOWMAN—Someone good at creating events that draw large crowds.

SUPERB—Of the highest quality.

SYNTHETIC—Made in a laboratory, not in nature.

TRADITIONAL—Done the same way from generation to generation.

Places to Go

ON THE ROAD

U.S. CELLULAR FIELD
333 West 35th Street
Chicago, Illinois 60616
(312) 674-1000

NATIONAL BASEBALL HALL OF FAME AND MUSEUM
25 Main Street
Cooperstown, New York 13326
(888) 425-5633
www.baseballhalloffame.org

ON THE WEB

THE CHICAGO WHITE SOX
  • *to learn more about the White Sox*

www.WhiteSox.com

MAJOR LEAGUE BASEBALL
  • *to learn about all the major league teams*

www.mlb.com

MINOR LEAGUE BASEBALL
  • *to learn more about the minor leagues*

www.minorleaguebaseball.com

ON THE BOOKSHELVES

To learn more about the sport of baseball, look for these books at your library or bookstore:

  • January, Brendan. *A Baseball All-Star*. Chicago, IL.: Heinemann Library, 2005.

  • Kelly, James. *Baseball*. New York, NY.: DK, 2005.

  • Mintzer, Rich. *The Everything Kids' Baseball Book*. Cincinnati, OH.: Adams Media Corporation, 2004.

Index

PAGE NUMBERS IN **BOLD** REFER TO ILLUSTRATIONS.

The Team

MARK STEWART has written more than 25 books on baseball, and over 100 sports books for kids. He grew up in New York City during the 1960s rooting for the Yankees and Mets, and now takes his two daughters, Mariah and Rachel, to the same ballparks. Mark comes from a family of writers. His grandfather was Sunday Editor of The *New York Times* and his mother was Articles Editor of *Ladies Home Journal* and *McCall's*. Mark has profiled hundreds of athletes over the last 20 years. He has also written several books about his native New York and New Jersey, his home today. Mark is a graduate of Duke University, with a degree in history. He lives with his daughters and wife, Sarah, overlooking Sandy Hook, NJ.

JAMES L. GATES, JR. has served as Library Director at the National Baseball Hall of Fame since 1995. He had previously served in academic libraries for almost fifteen years. He holds degrees from Belmont Abbey College, the University of Notre Dame and Indiana University. During his career Jim has authored several academic articles and has served in an editorial capacity on multiple book, magazine and museum publications, and he also serves as host for the Annual Cooperstown Symposium on Baseball and American Culture. He is an ardent Baltimore Orioles fan and enjoys watching baseball with his wife and two children.